Mister Lowry

by

John Caine

John Caine

MISTER LOWRY

*Eleanor.
With best wishes
JC.*

WRITE WORDS LIMITED

CAUTION

All rights whatsoever in this work are strictly reserved, and application for performance etc. by professional and amateur companies in all countries should be made before rehearsal to:

Sheil Land Associates Limited
43 Doughty Street
London
WC1 2LF

No performance may be given unless a licence has been obtained.

First published 2004 by:
Write Words Limited
78 The Green
Twickenham
Middlesex
TW2 5AG.
Copyright John Caine 1991

ISBN 0–9547507–0–5

Printed in Great Britain by:
Intype Libra,
Units 3/4,
Elm Grove Industrial Estate,
Elm Grove,
Wimbledon, SW19 4HE.

A C.I.P. record for this book is available from the British Library.

MISTER LOWRY is based on the life and work of the Lancashire painter, Laurence Stephen Lowry, who was born on the first day of November 1887 and died 23 February 1976.

"The essential key to a work of art is still a knowledge of its creator's life and how his mind worked."
Alistair Smith, Keeper at the National Gallery.

The author wishes to thank the Pirandello Heirs for their kind permission to use extracts from the play SIX CHARACTERS IN SEARCH OF AN AUTHOR, translated by John Linstrum and published by Methuen London Limited, and gratefully acknowledges the assistance given by Judith Sandling, Keeper of Art at Salford City Museum and Art Gallery and Shelley Rohde author of the Lowry biography, A PRIVATE VIEW published by William Collins Sons & Co.

MALCOLM TIERNEY, as Mister Lowry in the original
Bristol Old Vic production.
By kind permission of Bristol Old Vic.

MISTER LOWRY

The play received its world premiere at Bristol Old Vic on 9 December 1993, and was directed by Ian Hastings.

Mister Lowry was played by *MALCOLM TIERNEY*.

Designer Terry Brown
Lighting Lorraine Laybourne
Sound Mark Gallagher
Stage Manager Jo Weeks
Deputy Stage Manager Jo Matheson

For Carole, for her loving and unfailing support.

MISTER LOWRY

A PLAY IN TWO ACTS

ACT ONE: Scene 1

The parlour of the Lowrys' semi-detached Victorian villa, at 117 Station Road, Pendlebury.

It is late afternoon on a gloomy November day. As the house-lights go down we hear, softly at first, Chopin's Polonaise in E flat minor opus 26, number 2. As the volume of the piano music increases, a single spotlight is slowly brought up illuminating a worn chaise longue with two pillows at the head. Next to the chaise longue there is a small, circular wine table. On it are two clocks, a small bundle of documents including letters, bills and bank statements, and a few thin volumes of poetry. A gramophone stands on another small table. Downstage right there is an old, moquette-covered armchair. Next to it a small table. On the table there is a clothes' brush, an old exercise book containing press cuttings, and loose papers and books, one with a pince nez inside it. To one side is a wooden coat stand.

There are two matching dining chairs; one of them with a fringed shawl draped over its high back. A long case clock stands to one side. Elizabeth Lowry's collection of porcelain ornaments, and china cups and saucers is housed in a glass-fronted display cabinet, on top of which stand two more clocks. Upstage centre is Elizabeth Lowry's upright piano, the lid open as though ready to be played, with the music of a Chopin Polonaise spread open on the music rest. More sheet music is piled neatly on top of the piano, and underneath the piano stool.

A mahogany mantel clock and a carriage clock, stand on top of the piano. On the wall above the piano hangs Lowry's portrait of his mother. All of the clocks are in working order, and all show more or less the same time. The volume of the piano music reduces as the stage lighting is brought up gradually illuminating the parlour in the warm, amber glow of gaslight.

Now we can see that Mister Lowry is drowsing in the armchair, sprawled almost horizontal, his long legs stretched out in front of him.

Elizabeth Lowry's Voice Laurie! Are you there Laurie?
Lowry Yes mother. I'm here.
Elizabeth Lowry's Voice I've been on my own Laurie. Will you come and read to me?
Lowry Yes mother. I'm coming.

Lowry gets up from the armchair and crosses to the piano. He is a vigorous man, with short iron-grey hair and piercing blue eyes. His dark, three-piece suit is of good quality, 'though now shabby and almost threadbare. As always he has on a black tie, with a narrow gold pin holding together the points of a starched white collar, worn with a union shirt.

Pushed into the breast pocket of his jacket there is a white cotton handkerchief, which he occasionally pulls out with a flourish to rub his large nose. His wardrobe is completed with grey socks and heavy black shoes. He speaks with a Manchester accent and displays a sly sense of humour. His gestures are large and agitated and he walks quickly, with a curiously jerky, almost uncoordinated gait.

Lowry She's a beautiful pianist, with a fine talent . . . strangled by sickness. What she might have been, given good health. Mind you, Manchester was the capital of music in those days. The Hallé had just been formed, Grieg and Rachmaninoff came to give concerts in the Free Trade Hall . . . and Strauss . . . and of course Chopin. Mother did once play a concert at the New Islington Hall . . . Adolph Brodsky and Busoni appeared there. She plays as well as any concert pianist I've heard . . . but she wasn't blessed with the strength to match her ability.

He sits in the armchair, his legs stretched out in front of him, almost lying on the chair, and closes his eyes, lost in reminiscence. The piano music resumes and listening to it has an obviously relaxing effect on him.

Music is first of all the arts for me. Just listening to my mother playing the piano . . . she plays with such sweet clarity, you wished she'd never stop.

(*A sudden change of mood*)

She'd have preferred it if I'd taken a different road.
"If god gives you brains," she said, "it's your bounden duty to use them."

When I think back on all those years I wasted at school, the opportunities I threw away.

"Lowry," the head teacher said to me one day. "Lowry, you should put your head down the W.C. and pull the chain!"

(*With a rueful smile*)

Not a nice thing for the headmaster to say.

But I just couldn't see the purpose in schooling, not then, and when I could it was too late. Not one examination did I pass. There was one time I remember; the science teacher told me I was the living proof of Darwin's theory of evolution.

(*Pause*)

I thought it was a compliment. I rushed home after school to tell my dad. He was most put out . . . but then he was a Sunday school superintendent in those days. I think he was upset most that a teacher should speak such blasphemy.

As he talks he takes his trilby hat from the coat stand and brushes it carefully. Holding it by the crown between thumb and forefinger he places it on his head.

It's close to ten years since he died. February the tenth, it was, nineteen thirty-two.

A bleak day as I recall.

He takes his raincoat from the coat stand and puts it on. From a pocket in the coat he takes out a black armband and pulls it onto his left sleeve.

I was forty-five . . . though still living at home.

Well I had no cause to do otherwise. I wasn't married.

So it was left to me to look after mother . . . and this house, we rented.

A gloomy semi in Station Road, Pendlebury. Villas, they call them. Dad used to tell people he was Chief Clerk at Jacob Earnshaw's, but he did no more than collect rents for them, and penny insurances. Mother always says he was paid mostly in promises, and the Earnshaws had grown rich on his modesty. When I came home after the funeral . . . it was a damp, grey morning I remember, much like today. Standing in Southern cemetery, the wind got inside your clothes and seemed to seek out your bones. I was chilled to the marrow.

He blows on his hands, and rubs them together vigorously. Now we can hear the ticking of the clocks and the soft chimes of the mantel clock on the piano, joined by the chimes of the other clocks as they mark the hour. Lowry takes out his fob watch from his waistcoat pocket and holds it at arms' length, to compare the time it shows with the chiming clocks. He crosses to the table on which the documents are placed, and picks up the bundle of papers. Glancing through them he chooses one of the envelopes and looks at it. He searches distractedly through his pockets before finding his pince nez inside the book where he had left them. Adjusting the pince nez on his nose he studies the envelope.

This one's from Jacob Earnshaw's.

Taking out the letter he starts to read aloud from it.

". . . despite your many promises, we are disappointed to note that no payments have yet been made . . . therefore, we must insist that you repay the loan in full, on or before Friday the thirty first of March, in order to avoid further action . . .

He examines the postmark on the envelope.

He must have got this on the day he went out collecting, in that pouring rain . . . when we'd advised him against it. It seems he hadn't much option. It was his debts that drove him.

He continues to search through the various documents and comes across a tattered rent book.

There's no rent paid here for over ten weeks. He owes the doctor . . . and the gas bill; not paid.

He picks up a sheaf of bank statements.

And an overdraft . . . four pounds nine shillings and three pence.
He's lived next door to bankrupt for thirty years.

Amongst the papers he finds a sealed wage packet.

His last week's wage packet.

*He opens the small packet and slowly tips the meagre contents
into his hand. There is a small amount of silver and some cop-
per coins. We hear piano music, softly at first.*

(*Counting the coins*)

. . . six . . . seven and six . . . ten. Ten shillings and sixpence.

*Plainly distressed, he carefully reseals the envelope and takes a
few agitated paces about the room before crossing to the chaise
longue. Still holding the wage packet, he sits on the end of the
chaise longue and continues to look through the bundle of documents. As the music increases in volume, the general lighting
fades, leaving an amber spot on Lowry at the chaise longue. He
takes off his pince nez and rubs his eyes.*

Ten shillings and sixpence . . .

(*He stares, unseeing at the wage packet*)

Oh dad . . . dad.

*Taking off his raincoat he rolls it into a bundle before putting it
onto the seat of one of the dining chairs. He places his trilby hat
carefully on top of the rolled up raincoat.*

He was seventy-four when he died. A longish life you might say,
but not much to show at the end of it. No . . . he never amount-
ed to much, though he was cheerful enough, in his own way. It

was as though he'd been given a life to live, and he just got on with it

He started a clerk, and finished no better . . . yet he was a good man. Hard working and sober. His sobriety I've inherited, though I'm teetotal only because I'm afraid to take a little, in case it becomes a lot. Dad used to tell me stories about an uncle of mine who was finished through drink, so I never started. I did have a go at smoking . . . when I was twenty-two or three.
In my back bedroom with the door shut tight.
I fell asleep and woke up in a blazing bed with my dad banging on the door. I thought I was having a bad dream, till I smelt my hair singeing.
I've never smoked since.

He picks up the exercise book from the side table, and starts to leaf through it. He searches amongst the books and papers for his pince nez.

When I was going through father's things, after he'd . . . passed away, I found this book . . . filled with letters and cuttings he'd kept from newspapers. Reviews and notices of exhibitions where my work has been shown.

(*A change of mood*)

I had no idea he'd saved them. I never realised he'd taken that much interest . . .
I mean . . . he didn't show it . . .

Taking one of the cuttings.

This one's the first review that mentioned my name. It's from the Manchester Guardian, twentieth of February nineteen nineteen. Mister Taylor's review of the Annual Exhibition of the work of the members of the Manchester Academy . . . held at the City Art Gallery, Mosley Street.

(*He clears his throat before reading from the clipping*)

"There are good portrait heads by Messrs Barber, Roberts . . . and Lowrey."

(*Pause*)

Not given to lavish praise wasn't Mister Taylor.

And he spelt my name wrong. There's no "e" in Lowry. I can't fairly blame him though, seeing that's how it was spelt in the catalogue for the exhibition, and they managed to spell my first name wrong as well in that!

A few years back, I had one or two of my pictures shown at a small exhibition in Paris . . . they sent me a copy of the catalogue. They'd printed my name as, L.S.LOWSY.

Though you never know with the French . . .

(*A sly smile*)

. . . they might have been making a point. None of my stuff ever sold there.

He looks again at the clippings, before selecting another one.

The good old Manchester Guardian, they were always kind to me. They must have known my dad was a regular reader.

(*Reading aloud from the clipping*)

"November nineteen twenty one."

That was an exhibition I had with an architect called Mister Rowland Thomasson, and a friend of his, Mister Brown. They painted in watercolours, and we showed in Mister Thomasson's offices on Mosely Street. I used to call in most dinner times to see how it was going. I only worked round the corner. Most days there was just me and Mr. Thomasson in the place. One or two people might come in . . . passers by.

More if it were raining.

I read this notice so often; I had it off by heart.

(*Reading aloud*)

"Mister Laurence S.Lowry . . . both names spelled correctly . . . has a very interesting and individual outlook."

Art critics always call a picture interesting when they don't know what else to say about it.

"His portrait of Lancashire is more grimly right than a caricature, because it is done with the intimacy of affection. Mister Lowry emphasises violently everything that industrialism has done to make the aspect of Lancashire more forbidding than of most other places."

(*Pause*)

I'd no idea I was doing all that. I never dreamed it was me that was making Lancashire more forbidding. Still wouldn't, if they'd not told me.

(*Thoughtfully*)

That might be the best use for art critics. To explain to the artist what he's been doing.

I have no special affection for Lancashire . . . or anywhere else for that matter. I lived in Salford because that's where my parents lived, and I was too young to argue when they first moved there.

I painted what there was. In the country I painted trees and fields. When we went to the seaside, I painted the sea.

(*He returns to his reading*)

"Mister Lowry has refused all comfortable delusions. He has kept his vision fresh as if he had come suddenly into the most forbidding part of Hulme or Ancoats under the gloomiest of skies after a holiday in France or Italy." God knows how I did that.
I've never been to France or Italy. I've never been anywhere abroad in my whole life.
I went away with my mother in nineteen twenty-five, to Lytham St Annes

Doctor Simmons wouldn't let her travel after that; so I started going away on my own. I set out all over England. Previously we'd always gone to the Fylde coast . . . sometimes Rhyl.
I'm not attracted by abroad.
(*Looking again at the clipping*)

Just in case I was in danger of getting bigheaded, Mister Taylor put this bit in.

(*Reads aloud from the clipping*)

"The artist's technique is not yet equal to his ideas. If he can learn to express himself with ease and style, and at the same time preserve his singleness of outlook he may make a real contribution to art."

(*Sarcastic*)

And if he can at the same time earn a living, and fetch medicine to his bedfast mother, and make sure she's comfortable and gets her dinner . . . for all his clever words I didn't sell a single picture. But that notice was just what I needed at the time. It gave me a bit of confidence . . . the strength to keep on with what I was doing.

Leafing through the pages of the exercise book.

I never knew my father took such an interest in me. He never showed it . . . though he had little enough time . . . he did sometimes suggest subjects for me to paint. Places he'd seen on his rounds.

(*Pause*)

It's too late anyway. It seems that everything's always too late.

He closes the book and puts it back onto the table.

There was one article I do remember . . . and not because it gave me a good notice.

The FOH lighting fades to black. An outside door opens letting in the sound of wailing factory sirens and the clattering of clog irons on the cobbled street outside the house as mill workers make their way home. The door closes, reducing the volume of the outside sounds. From nearby we hear a clock strike six, echoed by the chimes of the clocks in the Lowrys' parlour. We can see Lowry moving upstage as the parlour lighting is slowly brought up.

June, nineteen thirty-three it was . . . not long after my father died. I'd just come in from work. Mother was more or less bedfast now . . . relying on me for most things . . . though we still had Ellen, and she was a great help. While the kettle boiled, I sat down to read the Manchester Evening News.

He is now sitting on one of the dining chairs reading the
Manchester Evening News.
We can hear the ticking of the clocks.

Elizabeth Lowry's Voice Is that you Laurie?
Lowry (*Continuing to read his newspaper*) Yes mother.
Elizabeth Lowry's Voice Will you bring up my cough mixture?
   I did ask Ellen, but you might as well talk to the wall.
Lowry (*Distracted*) Yes mother.

Suddenly he springs to his feet, staring at the newspaper.

(*He reads aloud with growing anger*)

"Academy honour for local artist. Two paintings by Laurence
Stephen Lowry, the Salford painter of Lancashire industrial
scenes . . . accepted by the Royal Academy for exhibition at their
annual show in London. Mister Lowry works at Pall Mall
Properties, the well-known Manchester estate agents, and he
does much of his painting in the evenings . . . art to Mister
Lowry is the antidote to a day of strain at his city desk."

(*Obviously hurt as well as angry*)

They have no right to print such monstrous statements. No right
at all. It's a rare treat this'll give those high falutin' members of
the Manchester Academy. I can just imagine them gloating
when they read it.

"Lowry? Isn't he the fellow who turns to painting as an escape
from the strain of his city desk?"

"He's an amateur . . . not a real artist . . . a Sunday painter."

The pleasure it will bring to those who dislike me, as much as
they despise my work.

(*He is deeply hurt*)

God knows I'm no amateur. Twelve long years I served at the life class . . . more than twenty years at Manchester College of Art. Surely I've learned my craft as long, as and longer than most of the so-called professionals. If I am a Sunday painter, then for me every day's Sunday.

(*His mood changes as he struggles into his raincoat*).

I'm going round to the Evening News offices, and I'll tell them plain, that I consider their article to be an outrageous and unwarranted intrusion into my private life. An artist is to be judged by his work alone.

A painting must hang on its merits.

He is stopped on his way out by the sound of his mother's voice.

Elizabeth Lowry's Voice Laurie. Will you fetch a cup of tea?
Lowry Yes mother. I'm coming.

As the parlour lighting fades to black, we hear the music of a Chopin Polonaise.

End of Scene 1

ACT ONE: SCENE 2

As the stage lighting is brought up, Lowry enters, carrying a leatherette shopping bag.
He takes off his raincoat and hat and hangs them on the coat stand

Lowry (*Dropping his shopping bag on the table*). Have you ever heard of anything as daft as that?

He fishes in the bag and takes out a few tubes of oil paint.

She says that oil paints are on ration. The silly old cow! "I can only let you have one tube of each, Mister Lowry. It's very scarce you know. I have to make it go round."

One tube per person. How the hell does she think that's going to help us beat Hitler?

(*His sly smile*)

Unless she stops selling Prussian blue.

Anyway, I got my own ration, then I sent Doreen in to buy more.

"Don't worry," I told her. "She won't ask you to prove you're an artist."

(*With an edge of bitterness*)

"You'd have a job trying to convince her that I was."

He sets out his tubes of paint on the table.

I'm a simple man, and I use simple materials, just a few

colours . . . ivory black, yellow ochre, Prussian blue and flake white. No medium. That's all I've ever used for my painting.

Watercolours I've tried now and then, but they dry too quickly. They don't suit me. I like to work on a picture . . . over a period of time. Well there's no need to rush.
No one's queuing to buy 'em.

He takes out of his shopping bag a small piece of cheese wrapped in grease-proofed paper.
He opens the wrapping paper and smells the cheese.

(*Pulling a face*).

My god but they hardly need to ration that.
There's nobody would want more than two ounces anyway.

(*Looking into the bag*)

No chocolate digestives of course.

With a sudden grin of triumph he takes out of the bag a small box of chocolates.

Cadburys Walnut Whirls. Two and six pence halfpenny
. . . and two months coupons.

He puts the box to his nose and greedily inhales the aroma before putting the chocolates back into the shopping bag.

Of course, if I had a wife I wouldn't have to do the shopping myself . . . and I'd have an extra ration of paint.

(*After a short pause*)

I'm not married.

Not that I haven't thought about it . . . often enough when I was younger . . . but I never could.

It got so as I used to worry about it. All around me, in the office, at night school . . . everyone seemed to be getting married. I knew they were : . . I was caught often enough for a subscription to one wedding present or another. My own wedding might have cost me a damn sight less than I was having to spend on other people's.
I got to thinking there might be something wrong with me.

In the end, I was so worried, I went to see a doctor . . . not that I've got much faith in the medical profession. They've done little enough that helps my mother . . . and even less for my father. Anyway, he put me through a most thorough examination . . . gave me every possible test.
When it was all done, there I was, still in my long johns, sitting on the edge of his leather couch. He was staring at me . . . very intently.
There was this long silence, and then he did a most hurtful thing. Looking me straight in the eye, he said.

"My god Mister Lowry, but you're ugly!"

(*With a smile*)

So I'm still single.
Though I don't know that I'm what you'd call a confirmed bachelor. I mean, I've got nothing against women, as such. And I suppose it'd be someone to talk to. But I'm well used to my own company, and I don't see as anyone else could grow into my ways, not now.

No, it's too late . . . it's all passed me by.

Besides, I've my mother still to think about.

There's only me that she'll let look after her now . . . though we've still got Ellen to help in the house, and her sister-in-law does the laundry. But mother complains Ellen can't lift her properly . . . and she has such awful bedsores. Me and Doctor Simmons have that job . . . and so long as I'm home in time to get her tea ready . . .

Aye, mother's got a lot to put up with, and not much to look forward to.

(*Thoughtfully*)

Young Doreen tells me I should get married.
I know there's folk older than me have done it. A married man they say, lives like a dog but dies like a king. A bachelor lives like a king and dies like a dog.

"But who'd marry a man like me?" I asked Doreen.

"My mam says there's plenty of women would be glad to have you, Uncle Laurie," she said.

An embarrassed pause.

She calls me Uncle Laurie. It was Doreen suggested it.

Well it's better . . . when we're out; with her being so young . . . she's almost sixteen, coming on twenty-six. She's so . . . sensible. And me being so very much older . . . she says it's better she calls me uncle. We were having a bit of tea in Sissons, and she said that she'd feel easier calling me "uncle". I laughed and told her I quite liked people thinking she was my girl friend . . . you can see them looking at us, wondering what's going on between us.
An old fogey like me with a pretty young girl . . . out together, just the two of us.

Not that she is my girl friend of course . . . well she is my
friend . . . and she's a girl . . . there's all sorts of friendships.

Being old doesn't mean you don't have . . . needs . . .

He stops in confusion.
Lowry crosses to the table and picks up his shopping bag. He
puts the bag on the arm of the chair and takes out the box of
chocolates.

We're going to see a play tonight . . . by Pirandello. At the Opera
House. It's called Six Characters in Search of an Author. I've
seen it before mind . . . seven times . . . no eight altogether. I saw
it three times in London. It's the only play that's ever really held
me . . . affected me.

They do fascinate me, those six figures in their black Victorian
costumes, moving together, slowly . . . and there's this young
girl in it, with long Pre-Raphaelite hair that falls across her
shoulders and down over her back. I've made two or three pictures of her.

They had to give her a rest after such a long run.

I wasn't so impressed with her replacement. But she'll be back
in it tonight.

Her mother knows of course. I mean Doreen's mother. She
knows I take her to the theatre . . . and the Hallé. I make sure she
knows . . . I make sure that Doreen tells her . . .

(*He laughs. A sudden, harsh laugh*)

. . . not that there's anything to tell . . .

(*Obviously uneasy*)

I mean, I do like Doreen. I enjoy her company. She might be young in years, but girls are sooner women . . . and women are too soon old. Well, round here they are.
Come next year, Doreen could be married; and tied with a string of skriking brats before she's twenty.

(*With sudden bitterness*)

Oh yes I've seen the looks. I've heard the sniggers from behind the grimy hands. But that's not how it is. Oh no sir. That's not at all the way it is.

The clocks start to chime. Lowry takes out a silver fob watch, holding it at arms' length to check its time against the chiming clock.

That taxi should be here by now.

Lowry struggles into his raincoat as we hear the sound of the doorbell. He brushes his trilby and lifts his foot onto a chair and polishes his shoe with the hem of his raincoat.

The doorbell rings again. Lowry remembers the chocolates and tears out a page from the exercise book and attempts to wrap up the box. A sustained ring from the door bell and we hear the voice of the young Doreen, calling through the letterbox.

Doreen's Voice Uncle Laurie. Come on, we'll be late. Hurry up!
Lowry (*Hurries to exit, clutching the half-wrapped chocolates*)
    All right Doreen. I'm coming!

We hear the piano music as the stage lighting fades to black.

End of Scene 2

ACT ONE Scene 3

The music fades to silence as Lowry enters. He is carrying a battered leather attaché case.
He takes off his raincoat and hangs it on the coat stand with his trilby.
We are aware of the ticking of the clocks.

It was March nineteen hundred and ten I started with Pall Mall Properties in Manchester . . . my father put me on to it. He said if I looked after it, I'd have a job for life.
"The work will give you your subjects," he said, "and the free time to paint them."

Not to mention the regular money.

(*He closes his eyes*)

Thirty-one years ago . . . it doesn't seem possible.

(*With a shy pride*)

I'm Assistant Secretary now, so my work is mainly in the office . . . looking after the books and ledgers. You know, you can see the whole of a life set out in a ledger. Credits and debits, the good and the bad. Remember your bank manager's your one true friend.
At least you know he values you only for your money.

And always put a bit by. Not like my poor old dad.

He is pacing the stage.

Chased to his death by creditors. Two hundred and fifty pounds he owed to the Earnshaws . . . and he'd even borrowed from his own nephew. Then there was the overdraft . . . and the bills.

He'd made a will leaving mother five hundred and thirty four
pounds four shillings and five pence . . . the amount of his insur-
ance policies drawn in her favor.
But he'd already borrowed against them for more than their
worth.

Still, I've managed to settle everything, and I've got a few
pounds behind me. Well, you don't want to end up buried by
strangers, a charge on the parish.

*He suddenly stoops and takes off his right shoe. He puts his
hand inside the shoe and examines the sole of the shoe carefully as he continues to talk.*

I do still collect a few rents. I have to, now that the younger men
are in the forces . . . young Openshaw's been called up.

*He has found the hole in his shoe and now he picks up the exer-
cise book and tears off the back cover. He folds it into a size and
shape to fit inside the shoe. Putting on his shoe he walks jerkily
up and down to test his 'repair'.*

He's in the air force, somewhere near Blackpool.
I told him he'll be safer there than he would be at home, what
with the air raids we're having here.

(*Almost defensively*)

Doing his collections gets me out and about, and I can stop as I
like and do a quick sketch . . . just as a note really, a reminder.
You won't catch me doing any painting outdoors.

That's all very well in France, where there's a bit of sunshine.
It's different again in a Manchester drizzle.
No, I can see no cause to give up my job. Besides, I've only got
eight years to my pension.

We've got Kathleen in to replace young Openshaw. Kathleen Hamer.

She's fifteen . . . nearly sixteen.

She came to us straight from school. It was a bit strange at first, having a female around the place . . . it's a long time since we had a girl in the office. When the last one left I remember she took the petty cash box with her.

Kathleen's a pleasant girl.

She's very . . . attractive, though she wears a bit too much powder and paint . . . I tell her, with her looks she wants no artificial help. No need to gild the lily.

We went to the Hallé on Sunday. Brahms Number One. She said she liked it . . . and god knows, her company's most welcome.

Though what pleasure she gets from an outing with an old man like me . . .

I've booked for us to see the Palace pantomime, that'll be more up her street . . . but she says it'll suit me better, judging by the sort of jokes I tell her.

He takes a pair of theatre tickets from his pocket and looks at them.

(*With sudden animation*)

'Dick Whittington and his Cat!'

We'll be there, in the Front Circle, twenty eighth of November . . . unless I get my call up papers first . . .

(*His sly smile*)

. . . though they'd need to be pretty desperate before they'll send for me to help them out.

I was called up in the last war . . . the Great War . . . the war to end all wars as they called it.
I didn't make it. When I went for my medical the army doctor did a few tests then sent me to a specialist.
He gave me a long examination. When it was finished he said he was sorry but I wouldn't be able to join the services. I didn't think to ask him why.

I was very lucky as it turned out.

It's a funny thing, but I saw that same specialist a few years back, at a private view. We looked at each other for a long time before it came to me who he was, and I was certain he wouldn't know me after all those years. He was staring at me, looking me up and down as though he couldn't believe his eyes, and then he said.

"Good god, are you still alive?"

Once again we become aware of the ticking of the clocks. Lowry stops to listen with us.

They're mother's clocks. She's collected them over the years.

One or two I got from clients.

(*Embarrassed*)

I bought them . . . from tenants needing money . . . I don't doubt some of them are valuable now.
But they all tell different times. You couldn't trust them if you've a train to catch.
And they're a bloody nuisance! Always needing winding or dusting.
You can have twenty different clocks, but there's only one sort

of time . . . and it goes just as quick, whether it's measured or not.

The ticking of the clocks grows louder.

Painting, so far as I'm concerned is devilish dull. There's no money in it. Plenty of bills in it.
That's where writers have the pull, a bit of paper and a pen and you're set.
They asked me if I'd like to have a go at writing . . . for the Manchester Guardian.
With Mister Taylor gone they thought I might like to do some reviews for them.

I don't think I'll bother. Painting's hard enough in itself, never mind writing about it.
Mother said the exhibition would be over long before I could get my notice properly phrased.

She's right. There's no sense taking on a distraction. Though writing is a skill I do admire and envy. The pictures they can paint with words, and fill with sounds and smells, as well as colours.

Lowry moves to the chaise longue and picks up one of the books of poetry.

Mister Rossetti could do both though. My mother likes me to read his poems to her.
This is one of her favourites.

(*Reads aloud from the book of poems*)

"Under the arch of Life, where love and death,
Terror and mystery, guard her shrine, I saw
Beauty enthroned: and though her gaze struck awe,

I drew it in as simply as my breath.
Hers are the eyes which, over and beneath,
The sky and sea bend on thee, - which can draw,
By sea or sky or woman, to one law,
The allotted bondman of her palm and wreath."

He rests the book on his knee.

Whenever I read that poem, I can actually see the picture . . .
though I don't much care for his subject paintings . . . but his
women. Rossetti's women are wonderful. I've found nothing
like them. Beautiful creatures they are. And those eyes . . .

"Hers are the eyes which, over and beneath
The sky and sea, bend on thee . . ."

Always know a genuine Rossetti by the eyes.
Other parts can be copied, but never those eyes.

(*His voice noticeably harsher*)

Of course, Rossetti's women are not real women.

Not the women you see round here, carrying shiny brown shopping bags. Worn-out women, pushing their pale faced babies in
big-wheeled prams. His women are dreams . . . the fantasies that
men have of women. Painted from models that were the most
ordinary of women in reality. In life they were grey-skinned
women, their fat arses streaked with blue veins . . . pendulous
tits still striped with the pattern of the brassieres they've taken
off and left behind the screen. You can bet the original Venus de
Milo was hourly paid . . . a shivering art school model, her nipples standing out like raspberries with the cold.
Her arms eaten off with frostbite.

(*A change of mood*)

There was a girl once . . . at art school . . . a clever young lady she was. Her name was Ann. She had long silk hair, the colour of ivory black, that she kept tied in a thick plait. Pulled back off her face, with a parting in the middle.
She lived in a farmhouse on Swinton Moss, a black and white house it was, that stood on its own and looked at Bolton across a flat moor of greyish green.
I found out later that her house was built in eighteen eighty-seven . . . the same year I was born.
I'd go with her to the railway station after class. We'd walk over the footbridge and wait for the train. I'd get off at Pendlebury . . . she'd stay on. We'd do that quite often. At the end of every summer I'd say to her, "See you next term." Then, one October, she didn't come back.

I never saw her again.

A few years since I went to Bolton . . . to make some enquiries. Her being so talented, I felt sure she would have been heard of. But I couldn't find any trace of her.
I would have liked to have seen her again. She didn't want to see me. She was wise; she'd given it up.

(*With sudden bitterness*)

Not for her the grinding struggle for artistic fame and fortune. She'd turned her back on all of that . . . and on me.'

Blackout. In the darkness we hear the opening bars of Mozart's Symphony number 40.

End of Scene 3

ACT ONE: Scene 4

*During the blackout a painting easel has been set down stage.
The music fades as the stage lighting is brought up. Lowry is
painting, his face and upper body hidden from the audience by
the easel*

I use this as my painting room now, since mother's taken to her
bed. Ellen complains about the paint that's splashed everywhere.
"There's more on the floor than there is on your pictures", she
says.

*Lowry steps from behind the easel and we see that he has on a
dark suit which is liberally splashed with white paint. He looks
ruefully at his paint-splashed jacket.*

I'd say there's more on my jacket.

He picks up two pieces of painting board.

A long time ago, as a sort of experiment, I painted a few pieces
of board with flake white, and then left them to see what passing time did to the colour.

*He places the boards on the armchair before standing back to
look at them. They are both painted with flat white, but one looks
considerably more yellow than the other.*

See.

(*Pointing to one of the boards*)

This one is new flake white. Six coats I put on that board, not
five weeks since.

(*He points to the other board*)

This is an old piece.

He turns the board over to look at the date on it.

This one I did eight years ago. The white's gone down. Like fresh fallen snow, in the city, draws its yellow colour from the sulphur smoke. My pictures'll look better years after I'm gone. I didn't start off painting on a white background. That's something else I have to thank Mr. Bernard Taylor for. Early on I took him one or two pieces I'd done of crowds in the streets in front of an industrial scene.

"This'll never do," he said, "you'll need to do better than that."

I'd worked very hard on them, so what Mister Taylor said came as a bit of a shock. He told me my figures were all mixed up with the background. The whole lot was too confused.

"Can't you paint the figures on a lighter ground?" he said.

"And how do I do that?" I asked him.

"That's for you to find out." he replied. "You're the one that paints them."

I picked up my pictures and came home.
I was very annoyed.
But I did two more paintings of figures on a white background. Just a plain flake white ground. That'll teach the old bird, I said to myself. I took them back and plonked them in front of him. He looked at them for a few minutes, then he said.
"That's what I meant. That's right. That's perfectly right."

I could have killed him. But that's how I've done it ever since.

My father was interested in my experiments with the painting boards . . . mother's more concerned with what I paint on them.

(*A long pause*)

She doesn't much care for my industrial sets. But she does like some of my work . . . the yachts I painted at Lytham Saint Annes. She likes those, and always says so. She's got such good taste . . . an eye for beautiful things. Like her clocks and her china.

She wasn't meant to be living round here. These aren't her proper surroundings.
Father could never appreciate her need for colour and light . . . not that he could have done much about it if he had.

"Why don't you do more of your seaside paintings?" She asks me. "Like those lovely sailing boats you did at Saint Anne's?"

I know she enjoys the soft colours . . . and she can't see my need to do my other pictures.
She mustn't be blamed for that. There's no one else can. She's just worried that I'll end up like my dad. But she's always . . .

(*Searching for the word*)

. . . interested. She always asks me how I'm getting on with my painting.

He crosses to the armchair and picks up the painting boards. We hear the music of Mozart's symphony number 40, growing in volume. Lowry crosses to the gramophone and takes off the record. He selects another record, which he cleans carefully with his sleeve.

I really don't know how I'd manage without music. It's the only thing that takes me to the other side.

He puts the record on the turntable and winds up the gramophone before placing the needle carefully at the start of the record.

Though I must say I'm beginning to prefer listening to music at home.

The music starts. It is Mozart's clarinet concerto. Lowry goes back to his easel and continues to work.

Audiences at the concerts are too distracting, coughing and shuffling . . . or else I find myself watching the cheeks of the trumpet player, wondering if they're going to burst and scatter his teeth amongst the fiddlers.

Mother enjoys listening to the music on the wireless I've bought her. She says it's a private pleasure.

He continues to work, with the sound of the music in the background.

I still can't do a cat. The only way I can paint a cat is by making a very bad dog, and then sort of decapitating it . . . then it becomes a cat.

An artist is an artist, no matter how he makes his daily living. Cezanne was nearly as old as I am now before he ever sold a picture. He lived on an allowance his father gave him.
So was Cezanne a professional? Or the Douanier Rousseau, the grand primitive, was he a real artist, a true professional? It seems you can paint for the length of a lifetime, and every day of the week, yet they'll still call you a Sunday painter.

He makes a sudden stab at the canvas with his brush.

There . . . I've operated on that one. Now he's got a wooden leg.

But I never put anything into a picture that I haven't actually seen for myself. These poor people, the cripples . . . they're all around us if you look for them.

Whenever I go out I watch for them, deliberately. I search out the maimed.
One day a friend of mine took me out in his car. We drove from Rochdale to Oldham, and on that single journey, I counted one hundred and one cripples.
Mind you it was easier for me to count, since I wasn't driving, so I could keep watch on both sides of the road.

Then there was another time, on a bus ride from Salford to Bury, I counted ninety-five.

I'm much more interested in these people, the cripples and the under people. They have a deep comic quality . . . that's not to say that they're funny, to hold them to ridicule; but painting what is there, what I see . . . and what anyone else would see if they troubled to look.
I don't paint them so as you could actually recognise a particular person, that would be wrong, and cruel.
No, I'm painting the condition, the tragedy that afflicts them, that grinds them deeper down, but never beats them.
I do feel very strongly about these people.
They are real people, sad people, and I find I'm attracted to sadness . . . and there are some very sad things.
I feel like them.
My cripples are really the wounded soldiers, injured in the great battle of life. That's how it is.
No sir, there's no place for sentiment in painting.

He continues to paint as the lighting fades.

It's the factories that crippled 'em. Most of 'em. The mills makes 'em deaf. The iron foundries smash their limbs. The places they get their living takes their life off them, a bit at a time. But the factories have a beauty of their own, and I was inspired by their beauty. At first when I was young, I didn't see it.

We had a French art teacher at night school. Mister Valette . . . Mister Monsieur we called him. He was an impressionist painter . . . "paint the light, take your easel out of doors," he told us.

I used to go out into the country sketching landscapes and the like. A farm on the Fylde coast, I remember. Sail boats at Lytham Saint Annes. I don't know about the light, but I do know it was bloody cold. The wind used to whip off the sea, across the beach and fill your ears and mouth with fine sand. Aye. Impressionism might be all right in France.

They've got the weather for it.

Then one day, a long time ago, I was walking with a man, in Salford, and he said look. And I looked, and I saw it . . . properly. And it changed my life.

It came to me that there was a brutal kind of beauty in the narrow-eyed mills.
And it was a natural beauty, borrowed off the granite they'd been made from.
And behind them the looming light . . . yellow grey . . . washed with a sort of veil of fine rain.
From then on I've devoted myself to it, and I've never tired of looking. It's always fresh.

Lowry crosses wearily to the armchair. He seems tired and list-less In fact he is exhausted by the strain of working and looking after his demanding mother. The music fades.

I'm plagued with carbuncles.

(*Pause*)

One or two of them in very inconvenient places. I've been to see Doctor Simmons, and he thinks it's because I'm trying to do too much, what with being short staffed at the office, and then having to come home and look after mother . . . not that I mind that in the least.

She prefers me to do things for her, and I'm glad if I can make her life a bit more comfortable.
The doctor says the carbuncles are a sign that I'm run down and I'm to take things easy. Naturally, he didn't bother to explain how I'm to do that exactly.
(*He is thoughtful*)

My cousin May did offer to come and stay . . . to help out she said. But she wanted to bring her bloody cat, and I couldn't have that . . . oh no, not cousin May's cat. I used to go to her house sometimes . . . straight from work, and stay for my tea, and there was this cat. She called it Charles . . . but it turned out to be female . . . truly a wild cat. Cousin May had tamed it by leaving bits of food on her back doorstep. She's supposed to have a diploma in domestic science, but I defy anyone to eat one of her cakes.

Even her wild cat wouldn't tackle one.

I was quite fond of that cat, but it disliked me intensely . . . and when it wasn't flying at me trying to scratch or bite me, it used

to sit . . . just sit . . . and stare. She used to look at me, so . . .
contemptuously, that I felt most uneasy. That cat understood.
Every Christmas I sent her a card with a pussy cat on, to try to
pacify it, and last year I sent her a really beautiful one.
Unfortunately, I forgot to send one to cousin May, and now I'm
in deep disgrace, so she probably wouldn't come even if I asked
her.
Anyway, it'd be awkward for me. Having two women in the
house.

(*Pause*)

Three if you count the cat.

We hear the music of a Chopin polonaise and the lights fade to
blackout. The music fades as an amber spot is brought up slow-
ly on Lowry. He is sitting on the chair at the foot of the chaise
longue illuminated by the single spot, which leaves the rest of
the stage in darkness.

He is talking to his mother as though she was still alive and
in her usual place on the chaise longue. He searches in his
pockets and unearths several envelopes, most of them unopened.
He sorts through them before he finds the one he is looking for.
Taking out the letter from the already-opened envelope, he finds
his pince nez, puts them on and starts to read it to his mother.

I'm to have my own show mother . . . a one-man show, in
London. Not in any old gallery either. My show is to be in St
James . . . the Lefevre, and Mister McNeil Reid says he'll use
the pictures that I've got at James Bourlet.
I told him . . . and Miss Jewell, that I couldn't possibly let them
have twenty five new ones by January next . . . it's already
November . . . and I'm tired . . . I'm so bloody tired.
So I suggested eight or ten fresh ones, with the rest to be chosen
from those I have at Bourlets for framing. A small show, say

twenty four, or twenty five in all. I have Miss Jewell to thank for all this. She'd left a small picture of mine on a chair near to her desk, knowing that Mister McNeil Reid was to visit her.

Reading aloud from the letter.

"He asked me who L.S.Lowry was, and I said he's a Manchester artist. Then he asked me to send half a dozen of your paintings to the gallery, and if his partner liked them as much as he did, then we'll have a show."

Miss Jewell said she's been sending my pictures to shows for years. They're always hung . . . and they always come back

Searching again in his pockets.

She's sent me a list of important people who are to have invitations to the private view . . . some London critics that I'm to invite personally.

Examining the list

I'll not be sending one to Mister Michael Ayrton. He said my stuff's revolting, and my people look the way they do because I can't draw the human figure. Twelve years drawing from life, twenty years of study, fifty-four years old . . . and still it's not enough for them.

Nor for you mother. Why don't you, just once, tell me that you can see what I've been doing?

Thirty years the people in Pendlebury have laughed at me.
And in Manchester, they've sneered and smirked behind their hands.

"Lowry? Oh he's just an amateur . . . a Sunday painter you know."

None of it would have been half as bad if you could find one word of approval . . . to hear you say, just once, that you like my work. I don't mean the yachts at Saint Annes . . . though they have their place . . . but those pictures I had to paint, else no one would.
I don't try to make them sordid or squalid, I paint them as they are . . . and there's beauty in it.
Real beauty.

But it's the people. A country landscape is well enough without people, but an industrial set is a shell, without people, an empty shell.
A street isn't a street without people . . . it's as dead as mutton! And it's the combination of the two . . . the mills and the people . . . and the composition's incidental to the people. The railways and the factories, the mills and the warehouses . . . they're just the background.
Sometimes I dislike them myself.

Yet as soon as I start, what happens?
Those pitiful-looking people swarm around the gloomy factories, and crowd the streets under their smoking chimneys. I stare at a blank white canvas and that's what I see, and that's what I have to paint. I can't help my pictures.

We can hear the second movement of Mozart's Symphony number 40 in G minor.

They must be done, though no one wants them.
I can't expect people to buy them; they didn't ask me to paint them.
They don't want my style of painting. They won't spend good money to be faced with a mirror of their own poor lives. Why

should they? Folk that buy paintings don't live in these streets anyway. They make their money here so they can live in greener parts.
Nice sunshine pictures they want for their walls . . . not my industrial sets.

Two hundred guineas someone paid for that country scene by Mister Barber that hung with mine at the Manchester Academy.
Two hundred guineas!
No one bought mine . . . even at four guineas.

The music grows louder. Lowry is crying with anger and bitterness.

Now I'm to have my own show . . . in London.
That's what I wanted you to see, mother . . . but you couldn't wait.

Why didn't you wait?

The next words emerge in a strangled scream.

Why wouldn't you wait to see my show?

The music stops suddenly as the spotlight is cut.
In the sudden blackout we hear a Chopin polonaise played softly at first then growing in volume.

End of Act 1

ACT TWO: Scene 1

As the houselights fade to black, and the stage lighting is cross-faded with them, we hear the music of Mozart's symphony number 40 in G Minor; softly at first and slowly increasing in volume.

We are in Lowry's painting room at "The Elms", his house in Mottram-in-Langdendale.

Most of the furniture has been brought from Station Road, though it is now looking much shabbier. Lowry's easel is centre stage, encrusted with splashes of dried paint. There are several partially completed canvases on the floor, and others propped against the foot of the easel. Paintings are scattered around the room, and leaning against the few pieces of furniture. Prominent amongst the various paintings is one of Lowry's "red-eyed" self-portraits.
The chaise longue from Station Road is stage left, covered in papers and books.
Stage right is the old moquette-covered armchair, which was set down stage in Act One.
The clocks are placed around the room, and on the walls we can see several paintings, including Rossetti's 'Proserpine' and 'Pandora', and works by Ford Madox Brown,
'The Parting of Herwig and Gudren' and 'Moses and the Brazen Serpent' We can also see paintings by Daumier, Lucien Freud, and Lowry's own portrait of his mother.

On the oval dining table, there is a large, ceramic fruit bowl. Lowry puts all his correspondence into this bowl, and it is filled with envelopes of assorted shapes and sizes, many of them unopened. Also on the table there is the gramophone from Station Road, and gramophone records are piled underneath the table on which are set various books, heaps of papers and draw-

ings. A standard black telephone is almost buried beneath the papers.
Behind the now cracked panes of the glass-fronted cabinet, which stands in one corner, Elizabeth Lowry's collection of china and porcelain ornaments is displayed, neglected and dusty. The two dining chairs from Station Road and the coat stand from Act One, complete the essential furniture. The music fades and mixes into a scratchy recording of the sextet from Lucia di Lammermoor as the stage lights come up.

Lowry is working at his easel. He applies each brush stroke with great deliberation, referring now and then to a sketch, which he has previously pencilled on the back of an old manila envelope. He is absorbed in his work.

Lowry Lately, I find myself thinking more and more about my own funeral . . . no . . . it's not a totally morbid subject. In fact it's very interesting. I often imagine what it will be like . . . oh I know I'll be there soon enough . . . in a passive capacity.

I once made a painting of my funeral. In my picture the hearse is a most beautiful job, all shining lacquer with etched glass panels. It's pulled by four brushed black horses, nodding their great ostrich feather plumes, their harness brasses worn thin from polishing. And the undertaker . . . there he sits, plump and smug on the box seat, smoking a big fat cigar . . . to celebrate the order. It's a Manchester day, a grey day . . . everything blurred with a thin drizzle blown across the empty cemetery. There's no one there to see my funeral, except the undertaker . . . and my solicitor. And when he thinks no one's looking, he lifts the cuff of his soft leather glove, sneaking a look at his wristwatch . . . keen to be away to his football match.

And why shouldn't he?
Once they've seen you nicely nailed up in your wooden cot, there's not much more even a lawyer can get out of you.

Southern Cemetery, that's where I'll be buried . . . next to my
mother. She . . . passed away the month after the war started. I
was fifty-two. They said it was a blessing.

She'd suffered for most of her life from bronchitis . . . the only
medal they pin to your chest for living in Salford.

*We hear the hissing sound, which indicates that the needle is at
the end of the track.*
Lowry crosses to the gramophone and lifts off the needle arm.
He takes off the record and replaces it in its sleeve.

And Doctor Simmons was no help.

(In a doctor's voice)

"It's the soot, and the factory fumes Mrs. Lowry. There's only
sickness flourishes in this dank air. You'd be better to move to a
more conducive climate."

Isn't that just typical of the medical profession? Prescribing as
the only cure, a medicine their patients can't afford. Doctors!
They're just like lawyers. They both charge a fortune for an
opinion that's certain to benefit them . . . but'll more than likely
prove expensive or fatal for their client.

(With a smile that indicates there's a joke coming)

They say there's a lawyer called Mister Strange buried in
Southern Cemetery, but the stonemason forgot to carve his name
on the tombstone, so it just says;

"Here lies an honest lawyer."

And everyone that reads it says, "That's Strange."

He is searching amongst the canvases stacked by the easel.

I don't know where that painting got to. Probably buried in the basement of some art gallery.
There's far too many fine pictures hidden in the cellars of public galleries.
Paintings are made to be seen.
A picture's only alive when someone's looking at it.

I moved here in nineteen forty seven, when I was sixty-two years old. I was forced to leave Station Road the landlord claimed he wanted the house for his own use, so he had me thrown out. Mr. Bennett found this place for me, and his bank arranged a loan . . . so I bought it. Sixty-two years old and buying my first house . . . just when most people are thinking of retiring.

I've come too late to everything in life.

In those days, Mr. Bennett was assistant manager at the London and County Westminster in Spring Gardens . . . where I had what bit of money the government let me keep.
He commissioned a picture from me, very early on. One of my street scenes he wanted, with lots of people and . . . dogs. Five pounds was all he could afford, so I did him one . . . for five pounds . . . unframed of course. He's the Reverend Geoffrey Bennett now.

He's stopped telling folk how to save their money, and he's teaching them how to save their souls.
I told him this house would be no good for me, being so far out in the country. I've lived all my life in the town. I said I'd find it too quiet to get to sleep.

It wasn't as though I was looking for a place to retire . . . dear me no . . . I couldn't afford to retire, nor am I ever likely to, not with the income tax I have to pay.

Lowry sits in the armchair, legs splayed out.

Dear me no. I'll die in harness, just like my father. I'm resigned
to it.
Working like a galley slave to the bitter end. It's a house that's
everything I didn't want. I fancied large rooms and these are
small. I needed to be close to the railway station . . . and I'm
more than three miles away.
I've never learned to drive, even if I could afford a car, so I
wanted a decent taxi service on the doorstep . . . the nearest is
four miles away. But I can't move again, it's too much trouble.

I get fed up . . . on my own, stuck out in the wilds.

Mr. Bennett came to see me one day, only a few weeks ago, and
I'd got all my drawings stacked up in a pile out in the garden.

"Come on in," I said to him, "you're just in time to see the
bonfire."

"What bonfire?" he said.

Then I took him in the garden and showed him the heap of drawings I'd made.

"I'm going to set fire to the bloody things" I told him, "I'll burn
the whole dammed lot."

"You're not going to burn them," he said.

"Yes I am. They're no use to me. I'm sick of it."

Oh aye. I was deadly serious . . . and that would have been the
end of me. The reverend gentleman was most upset, and said he
would find the money to buy them from me.
But I wouldn't take anything for them.

He crosses to the gramophone and selects a record, which he takes out from its cover and wipes carefully with his sleeve, before placing it on the turntable.

He's got them in his house to this day. He's got more of my pictures than I have . . . when they want an exhibition of my work, I tell them to go to him. A London dealer offered him seven thousand pounds for those drawings not so long ago, so they must be worth a lot more.
But the Reverend Bennett won't sell . . .

(With a wry smile)

. . . well, not 'til after I'm dead.
We hear the music now from the gramophone. Brahms' Symphony Number One.

Mother was eighty-four when she went . . . old enough to die, but too young to want to. I do miss her . . . I often feel that she's still with me. Sometimes, when I'm painting late at night, I fancy I can hear her calling to me, asking me to come and read to her.

He crosses to the table and picks up a volume of poetry.

She used to like me to read to her . . . poetry was her favourite. She'd lie back in her pillows and close her eyes, and I'd read something from Wordsworth or Rossetti. You could see the lines go from her face and the pain soothe away. But she left too soon . . . before she could see how it was turning out.

The lights have been dimmed.

It wasn't so bad when my father died. I still had mother, and she needed me.

And it was only me she wanted at the end. But now there's no one. No one left.

If I'd got married. Course I couldn't. Not with dad's financial problems . . . and mother being so poorly. Then . . . it was too late. What sort of catch was I then? An impoverished old painter. I've got nothing against women. There's one or two I would have married. If they'd have had me.

We hear knocking on the front door. The music stops.
More knocking and then a young girl's voice

Young Girl's Voice Uncle Laurie! Uncle Laurie! Open the door Uncle Laurie.
It's me, Maureen. Come on. Open the door.
Lowry Be patient child! I'm coming! I'm not as young as I used to be.

She's a bright girl, and very pretty. She calls in sometimes . . . on her way from school.

(Embarrassed and defensive)

I'm helping her with her drawing. She's hoping to go to Art College. I call her child, but she's a young woman really. She's nearly sixteen. Her mother brings me my dinner sometimes. It's the least I could do.

The doorbell rings

All right Maureen. I'm coming.

As he crosses to exit, the lighting fades and we can hear Brahms' Symphony Number One.

End of Scene 1

ACT TWO: Scene 2

The music fades as the lighting is brought up on the easel where Lowry is working. He has taken off his jacket but still wears his waistcoat, complete with watch chain, and his collar and tie. The music has stopped and we can hear the ticking of the clocks. One of them chimes twelve. Lowry takes out his pocket watch, which he holds at arm's length to check the time.

He looks at the chiming clock and shakes his head before crossing to the gramophone and turning over the record. He returns to his easel as the music of Mozart's Symphony Number 38 in D Major begins. As he works he talks to the painting.

A Sunday painter they call me Mr. Bennett. Not a real painter at all . . . not a professional artist.
I don't paint shadows in my pictures, that's how the experts can tell a painter who works at night, after he's finished his paid job. Working in electric light they say you can't get the shadows right. I've fooled the bloody know-alls Mr. Bennett.

It's gaslight I work in.

(Intent on his work)

And here's my lovely Ann, thinking her own thoughts . . . lost in her own world . . . and who's this watching you while you play? This can be your uncle . . . your father's far away.

He might be dead, but don't be sad.

I'll see you won't be alone . . . not now Ann . . . no more a lonely, only child. You did right to give it up. But I do wish you'd said. I did come looking for you.
But I knew you didn't want to see me. It might have worked out

all right, if you could have waited. My mam's gone. I'm on my
own now Ann.

There's no one else.

The music starts to fade.

Oh I've got plenty of acquaintances. There's hundreds of people
seek me out . . . many more since my name's been well known,
and the price of my pictures has gone up. Never a soul did I see
when I was living like a monk in Pendlebury.
Not a living soul did I see then, from one week to another.

*The music stops. Lowry picks up a handful of envelopes from the
bowl.*

Now I get letters from people I've never even heard of, all of
them wanting something of me . . . a small drawing or sketch, or
like this one . . .

He selects a blue envelope and takes out the letter.

. . . would I be able to help her daughter who wants to be an artist
and has a lively talent. Some claim to be long lost relatives . . .
a second cousin twice removed, who's never really forgotten
me. Now I don't even open them.

*He throws the envelopes back into the bowl retaining the blue
envelope, which he puts into his pocket.*

I leave all my letters in there.
If it's something important they'll send me a telegram.
Some envelopes I do open. Those with cheques in. I always
open those.

Any that look to be official, usually income tax, I leave those in a separate pile for the accountant to deal with. People who know me put their name on the back of the envelope when they write to me, so I'll know to open it. Anyway, I don't have the time to read all the letters I get, and if I did then I'd need to waste even more time answering them.

But then they come knocking on my door.
Everyone wanting something, and mostly for nothing.

One day, there was this woman came to see me . . . out of the blue, just turned up knocking on my door. She had a drawing she wanted me to look at, one of mine she said it was, that she'd paid fifteen pounds for ten years ago . . . and that was a lot of money in those days. But it wasn't signed and she wondered if I'd sign it for her.
Well as soon as she showed it to me I knew it wasn't right, it wasn't one of mine, but I felt sorry for her, paying out all that money for a fake, so I signed it anyway.

(With a smug grin)

That'll be a problem for the experts. A fake picture with a genuine signature.
Does it bloody matter? A picture's a picture. If you like it, then it's real.

Forging my cheques I'd look on as serious.

If someone wants to spend his time trying to copy my work, then let him do it. He'll be disappointed though. When he does manage to draw like I do, they'll tell him he can't draw at all.
It goes to show what a sham the art world is. Run by dealers who know all about money and nowt about art. On the say so of the critics, who know nowt about neither.

Ben Johnson that said a man who writes other than for money is

a fool? He did that . . . and so did I. Oh I've been a dammed fool.
Most of my work's been given away. My father used to give my
drawings to Ellen, a servant girl we had, instead of wages. Mind
you, her mother was a sensible woman; she didn't spend more
money having them framed. She took them to the pawnshop and
drew cash for them . . . not that she'd get much for them in those
days.
I see paintings of mine I was glad to get four guineas for, changing hands for hundreds of pounds . . . and where's the benefit to
me?

That's the work of the dealers . . . the commission men.

No sane man should contemplate art as a way of life, certainly
not as a way of making a living. A regular monthly salary and
lots of time to paint, that's the ideal.

So far as I'm concerned, whatever financial rewards there may
be are shared between the tax collector and the dealers.
How the hell can it be considered fair that I should pay so much
tax now, after the years and years that I never earned a penny
piece from my painting?

(With increasing vehemence)

How can it be right that a dealer should make more profit from
the sale of a picture than the artist who painted it? How would
you feel if you saw a painting that you'd sold for five pounds
when you were unknown, changing hands for hundreds . . .
thousands of pounds . . . and none of the profit coming to you?
I have learned to be wary of the middlemen.
Without talent of their own, beyond the knack of making money
from other men's work, they grow fat through the industry of
poor painters like me.
My god, but I know how the racehorse must feel when it stands

there whipped and sweating after a race, and watches the smirking owner collecting the prize.
But I learned, oh yes I've learned.

Another time, when someone knocked on my door, it was a big London dealer. I went to the window and saw his posh car outside. Just passing through he said he was, and thought he'd call on the off chance that I'd be in, to talk about a wonderful deal he had for me.
A wonderful deal for me you notice, nothing in it that would be of any benefit to him of course. He said if I'd let him have the rights to print seven hundred and fifty copies off one of my Lancashire scenes, he'd stand the cost. Then he'd pay me to put my signature on all of them.
Well, after a bit of an argument, it was agreed that I'd get three pounds ten shillings for every print I signed. An amount that I thought was small for the job, and he claimed was exorbitant.

Two or three months later he was back, with a great bundle of prints under his arm.
He plonked them on the table and gave me his gold pen.
I asked him for the cheque. He handed it over; with some reluctance I might say, making a great fuss about the amount I was getting, for the little I was doing.
I saw straight away that it was less than we'd agreed for the job.

I didn't say anything and he laid all the prints on the table and I started to put my autograph on them, only I was signing them all, L.S.Low. After I'd done a few, with the dealer watching over my shoulder, he suddenly said. "What's this Mr. Lowry?"
You should have seen his face. "This is only half of your signature," he said.

You've only given me half my money, I told him.

(He laughs at the memory)

A lot of the art snobs complain about me signing prints.
They reckon that proper art shouldn't be sold in furniture shops.

He is looking through the drawings on the table.

We all know what's behind that. It's just the art dealers, worried
that they won't be getting their pounds of flesh. I know what I'm
doing. If someone's prepared to pay more than its value for a
cheap, coloured print, just because I've signed it, that's up to
them.

My bank manager thinks it's money for jam. And he should
know.
In time the prints'll be seen for what they are, autographed pho-
tographs . . . worthless.
My paintings will survive.

*He crosses to the armchair and drops into it, his legs stretched
out in front of him.*
We hear the Mozart, very softly at first.

God I'm tired.

*He closes his eyes. The music swells as the lights fade to black.
The telephone rings, cutting off the music. The lights are
brought up slowly to full. The telephone continues to ring for
some time before Lowry gets up from the armchair to answer it.
He searches through the papers and books to pick up the receiver, just as the ringing stops.*

They went on at me to get this dammed machine put in. Living
on my own, at my age, they said it would be better . . . in case
of an emergency. Though I give no one my number, there's
plenty seem to find it . . . and they never ask permission to ring
me up.
I've asked the telephone people to come and fix it so that I can

call out, but it'll not take incoming calls. If it's my emergency, then I'll be the one to make the call.

Lowry starts to paint, referring to a small pencil sketch he has made on the back of the blue envelope he has taken from his inside pocket.

When I'm outdoors, and I see something I fancy doing, I just look at it for a long time and make one or two small sketches. I use a bit of paper, or the back of an envelope.

He looks at the blue envelope in his hand with a slightly puzzled expression. He takes out the letter and reads aloud.

"I do hope you will not be offended by my writing to you like this, but with our name being Lowry, as yours is, and spelt in the same way exactly, I wonder if there's some family connection. There aren't any other Lowry's I know of with our spelling. Only four in the whole telephone book . . . and all of them spelt with an "e". But it's really about my daughter that I'm writing, Margaret whose just coming up to fourteen and seems to have a real talent for art . . . which is another reason I believe we might be related, since it's none of us she gets her talent from."

He looks up from his reading.

No doubt a second cousin twice removed.

He resumes his reading.

"As she has no father at home, and money is scarce from my work as a weaver, there is no chance for her to go to art school. But if you would have any time to look at her drawings to advise me . . ."

He puts the letter back into the envelope.

I've got no time to be looking at the doodlings of a young girl, even if her name is Lowry.

My father's name was Lowry, but it gave him no special ability to paint.

No, Mrs. Lowry. I think it's my money you're after . . . and an easy life for your daughter, and no doubt for yourself.

Lowry puts the envelope into his pocket.

(Smiling)

I can't imagine my mother ever writing to someone to promote my talent, even if she'd believed I had any.

(Quickly covering up)

Though she always encouraged me to continue with my painting.

He crosses to exit.

I think it's time for a nice cup of tea . . . and a chocolate digestive.

That's if I've got any left since young Maureen's been. I told her you couldn't get chocolate digestives during the war. They were on ration.

"What did you do Uncle Laurie?"

"I did without." I said. "In this life, child there's lots of things you have to learn to do without."

She preferred to call me "uncle" . . . with her being so young, it seemed more natural, when we were out somewhere . . . together.

The lighting fades to black. As the lighting is slowly brought up, Lowry enters carrying a mug of tea and two chocolate digestives. He crosses to his armchair and sits dunking the biscuits in his tea.

My dad enjoyed a chocolate biscuit, when he could afford 'em. He weren't allowed to dunk 'em. Nor could I, not when mother was alive.
He didn't seem to mind being bossed. He was very easy going . . . anything for a quiet life. Though I don't doubt that mother had a lot to do with that. He let me be.
Dad was an estate agent, and every day he used to catch the bus to his office in Manchester, carrying his attaché case. My god, but that's something I never could have done.
The thought of going to the office every morning at nine, with your butties in your little case, then back again at six o'clock, collecting a couple of rents on the way. Forever repeating the same old routine, day after day, until one day, one Friday afternoon the boss hands you a gold watch and a little envelope.
Good god no. I couldn't imagine doing that.

He crosses to his easel and picks up a brush.

Of aye, there were times when I wondered if I'd ever make any money from my painting, but I was living at home so it didn't really matter. Every now and then I'd get fed up with it and tell myself it was ridiculous, and that I'd have to get a job.
But I couldn't stand the thought of the daily trip to an office.

Then, just when things were looking desperate some small sale would come along . . . there were always a few private buyers in Manchester . . . and that would keep me going for another year. So I stayed on at home . . . painting.

He is immersed in his painting.

How's that for a fine pair of tits, Mister Lowry? How d'you like them? I last saw a pair like those on that tottie in Sunderland. That silly tart that was asking me about my seascapes, and trying to tell me that my lighthouse was a phallic symbol. I told her. "If I wanted to paint a cock", I said, "I wouldn't waste my valuable time painting a bloody lighthouse."

But she did have a lovely pair of tits.

As he paints, we can see that Lowry is becoming more excited with his work, applying his brush in short, stabbing strokes to the canvas. We hear Mozart's Symphony Number 41.
Lowry is breathing in short, panting breaths, and speaks in short rhythmic bursts.

Oh dear me, Mister Lowry that is a very short skirt . . . very short indeed. I don't think Ann would wear anything as short as that you know. This can be our secret.
A picture no one else will see.
Dear me no, Mister Lowry.
No one must see this picture. Not till I'm dead and buried. It's just between us. It'd give them Royal Academy buggers a bit of a shock if they could see this one.

He is painting with genuine passion.

Oh god . . . what it's like to be driven in misery by the needs of my flesh, still alive with desire . . . and it is misery you know, unspeakable misery for the man who lives alone, and who detests sordid, casual affairs. Not old enough to do without women, but not young enough to be able to go and look for one without shame.

Each of us face to face with other men, is clothed with some sort of dignity, but we know, only too well all the unspeakable things that go on in the heart . . . everyone's like that, only some of us haven't the courage to talk about it.

Just look at your lovely, long hair . . . wound in a glossy plait . . . and here's your bow . . . a great big bow to tie up your bonny brown hair.

(Aggressively)

Now, we'll just tighten your belt . . . your wide shiny belt . . . like that, so that your tits push out . . . and we can see the shadows of your nipples . . . touch them, standing out . . . erect. Quiet. Keep quiet. I'll tie this bow round your neck . . . it'll be a collar to keep you . . .to hold you still.

He is working with enormous intensity, painting out his sexual frustrations.

No you're not Ann. You're Doreen. This is your little rounded arse, wrapped in your tight black skirt . . . that rides above your thighs and creases . . .

Lowry is beginning to break down. The music grows louder and he stabs at the canvas with his brush.

And here comes a chopper to chop off your head. Not really to cut off . . . oh my beautiful Ann . . . why did you go? Why did you leave me?

Why did you leave me mam? Just when I needed you most.

Why?

Now he is moaning, racked with long shuddering sobs and he falls into his armchair as the music reaches a climax. The music stops. Blackout.

End of Scene 2

SCENE 3

The music resumes, calmer now, and remains in the background as the lights are slowly brought up to reveal Lowry standing at the table. He is holding the telephone and dialling a number.

Lowry Hello? L.S.Lowry here. Are you there?
Is that you Mr. Mitchell? Can you hear me?

He speaks in the loud voice, and with the exaggerated enunciation of a man not used to talking on the telephone. The music stops.

I'm not well at all sir, not well at all.

Yes, that's why I telephoned; I'm coming up to Sunderland on Tuesday. Will you be able to meet us at the station?

Well there's someone coming with me, we'll be staying at the Seaburn Hotel if you won't mind booking the rooms for me.

(He listens intently)

Margaret. Margaret Lowry . . . yes, spelt just the same as mine.
We'll need two rooms . . . my usual one, facing the sea and another one . . . near to.
She's . . . she's my . . . niece, and very talented.

I reckon she'll be a very good artist one day.

(Embarrassed)
Fifteen . . . well, nearly sixteen. Old for her years.
No, I didn't know either. On my mother's side.
Evidently they lost touch with the family.
It was her mother, she wrote to me, then brought Margaret to see

me . . . to show me her drawings. We'll be staying for a fort-
night. Yes, we should arrive at about half past three.

I'm most obliged to you Mr. Mitchell. Oh, how's the exhibition
going? Not sold out yet?
No I've not seen the notices. The work will speak for itself
Mister Mitchell. Nothing anyone does, says or writes will make
one happorth of difference in the end.

Well, I'll say ta ta for now, I can't afford these long phone calls.

He puts down the receiver.

Why should I care what the so-called experts say? Arty
crafty . . . the longer the hair, the shorter the art. Anyway, I don't
like talking about art.

We hear the music of Brahms' symphony number one.

(His mood changes)

But I do like Sunderland, and the good old Seaburn Hotel.

And the cold grey sea that stretches out forever. I stand for hours
on the shore, just looking . . . you can't tell where the sea ends
and the sky starts, there's just the faintest smudge of dusty yellow light far out. And in between, the deep flat water. I stand and
watch, and wonder what would happen if the tide didn't turn
next time . . . if next time it just came on and on.

I often wonder about that.

I'll paint a seascape self-portrait.
I'll be a tall, straight pillar, standing up in the middle of the
water . . . waiting for the sea of life to finish it off. Some silly
sod would say it was a phallic symbol.

The music swells as the lighting fades to black.
As the lighting is brought up we see Lowry at his easel. He takes
up a brush.

Critics say I've turned my people into puppets, as if I were trying to show the hard economic necessity that drove them. To say
the truth, I wasn't thinking very much about the people themselves. I don't care for people the way a reformer does.
They're simply part of it, part of the work . . . part of the private
beauty that haunts me.

If I loved them, as they tell me my paintings show I do, then I
loved them in the same way that I loved their houses, and the
streets that they live in. And the factories that they work in that
take away their lives . . . a day at a time.
Aye. They were just as much part of the vision. No more and no
less.

But if I'd drawn them to be really the way they are, then it
wouldn't have looked like a vision. It would have been any-
body's view of Salford.

The whole of my happiness, and the cause of my unhappiness,
is that my view is like no one else's. If it had been then I
wouldn't have been lonely, yet if I hadn't been lonely, I
wouldn't have seen it the way I saw it.
What I did see, and what I painted, became my companion.
But no man can live just with his imagination. Though my painting is a support, it can't make my solitude less.
And as time goes on, I get more and more alone.

If it wasn't for my painting I couldn't live, but it's more of a
drug now than a pleasure.
Painting helps me forget I'm on my own.
I have friends, of course, and a lot of acquaintances but it's not
the same. There was a poem I used to read to my mother, by

Elizabeth Barret Browning, she had me read it to her so many times, I know pieces of it still, off by heart.

There's one verse that stays with me,
"O dreary life we cry oh dreary life,
And still the generations of the birds
Sing through our sighing. And the flocks and herds
Serenely live, while we are keeping strife."

His brushes and palette fall from his hands.

God but I'm tired.

Blackout and silence.
In the silence we hear a clock strike ten. The lighting is slowly brought up to reveal Lowry sitting in his armchair drinking tea and dunking his chocolate digestive biscuits.

Why is it that restaurants can't do a lightly fried egg?
Always, when I ask for egg and chips, I say to the waiter, "Will you please ask the cook to make me a lightly fried egg." I like the yolk to be a plump runny yellow, so I can dip my bread; with the white like crackly lace, crisp round the edges.
What you get is a cold flat thing, hard and dry and stiff as a board. No use at all for egg and chips. Even at the Seaburn they can't manage it, and god knows they've tried often enough now. But they do make a good meat and potato pie, with a thick brown gravy. A piece of their pie, with some mashed potatoes and a pot of tea; followed by bananas and cream . . . the queen herself couldn't have better.

And they looked after Margaret as if she was a princess.
On our last day they made her a lovely sherry trifle, because they knew it was her favourite. It's one of my favourites too; with lots of cream . . . double cream, good for babies and growing children.

He gets up and crosses to his easel.

Given the choice, I'd sooner have a nice meat and potato pie, than any picture ever painted.

Mister Mitchell tells me that I've been invited to have tea with the Prime Minister at Number Ten Downing Street. Evidently Mister Wilson thinks I'm a socialist, no doubt because I paint pictures of factories and working people.
He used one of my paintings for his official Christmas card.

He continues painting.

He didn't send me one.

No, I've never been a socialist . . . and never will be.

I paint pictures, not propaganda. I showed the tall chimneys and the people who lived in the gloom of their smoke . . . I painted them because they were there. Painting poor people doesn't make me a socialist; any more than painting sick people makes me a doctor. If you're to be a painter, then you must paint something.

No, I won't be going to Downing Street. If he wants to meet me he can come here.
He knows where I live.

The funny thing is Mister Heath offered me a knighthood when he was the Prime Minister.
He must have thought I was a Tory.
Politicians. They're all the same. Liars and incompetents. None of them fit for proper work.
Now if they'd offered me a Dukedom, with a nice fat salary, then I would have considered it very seriously.

Anyway, it's all too late . . . far too late.
For sixty years no one gave a damn if I were alive or dead.
A few bob then would have been appreciated. When I really needed it.

He puts down his brushes and crosses to exit still talking.

When I had a life to look forward to.
Now I never look forward. I live my life; such as it is, in the past.

He returns from the kitchen carrying a bowl filled with fruit and cream. He carries it to the armchair where he sits and eats.

It's a great mistake to live too long . . . you run out of people; and it's even worse to live too long on your own.
I did have close friends once, but they're all long since dead.
There's no one now.
Nothing left.
I just carry on from day to day.

He rises and crosses to the table where he puts down the empty bowl and picks up one of his paintings.

These people in my pictures . . . they're alone.
All of them with their private sorrows, but they can't make any contact with each other.

We're all of us alone, cut off . . . and crowds are the loneliest places of all. In a crowd, everyone is a stranger to everyone else, but pushed together in a kind of forced intimacy.
You've only got to look at them to see that.

I can't make my people look cheerful . . . they've not got much to be cheerful about. That's one of the saddest things . . . watching people trying to enjoy themselves. There's a sort of desperate determination about it, brave but futile.

He picks up a drawing.

Look at that poor child . . . all her life before her.

He crosses slowly to his easel. He is very tired.

Sometimes when I'm painting, it's as though I'm letting off steam. Like a dream, only I'm awake. It's a dream that I make up for myself. People say that dreams are really things we want to do, or what we want to happen. Our dreams set us free. In a dream you're able to fly, or play the piano at a concert with wild applause filling your ears.

I paint my darkest dreams.
Sometimes, when I'm working, late at night and on my own, a picture will seem to paint itself, as though it's determined to be seen. And when it's done, I feel as though a great weight's been lifted from my brain.
Late at night, that's the worst time. I paint through the loneliness, listening to my music and talking to the picture I'm painting. I sometimes wonder if I'm going mad.

Then I look at the dream I've painted and I don't know what it means, only that it wanted to be seen, but must be hidden.
This isn't any kind of life . . . I'm not meant to be alone.
No man should be sentenced to this daunting solitude.
The desire to do all the work has left me forever now.
I feel I'm at the end.
Living on your own is bad enough, but no man should have to die on his own.

Lowry moves slowly to exit as the lights start to fade.

It's a great mistake to build your life around your parents.

Blackout.

We can hear the sound of clocks ticking before the lights slowly start to come up. One of the clocks chimes, seven times. At first, as we begin to make out the shapes of the furniture, it seems as though the room is empty. Then we see Lowry, lying face down on the floor, clutching a bundle of unopened letters. He is eighty-nine years old, and very sick.

Now then Mister Lowry! This won't do you know.

Still lying prone.

This won't do at all. You've a lot to do today . . . come on now . . . up you get.

He crawls to the table.

You'll feel better when you've had some breakfast.

He grabs the table and pulls himself upright. Once he is on his feet, very unsteadily, he drops the bundle of mail into the bowl on the table.

Is it worth it? Was any of it worth the effort? For those who have lived their lives surrounded by their families . . . or like me, surrounded by the garden fence.
Eighty nine years . . . a long lifetime making pictures, and what's the good of it?
What's the use of art anyway? Fleeting, it's only been fleeting.

He examines one of his drawings.

No, it can't all have been a waste . . . not all of it.

Still looking at the drawing.

How did I ever do that? A lot of hard work in that.
Couldn't do it now.
Can't do it now, not now.

He lets the drawing fall to the floor.

I don't feel too good today sir, not too good at all.

The doorbell rings and Lowry struggles towards the exit.

Margaret Lowry's Voice Uncle Laurie! It's Margaret.
Come on Uncle Laurie, we're going to be late.
Lowry I'm coming! You must be patient. I'm not a young man
   any more.
My legs are stiff.

The doorbell.

I'm coming child. Don't be so impatient.

He stumbles and falls into the armchair.

Wait a minute will you?

*We hear the rattle of the letterbox, and the voice of a young girl
calling to Lowry.*

Margaret Lowry's Voice Uncle Laurie! Are you there Uncle
Laurie?
Lowry You must be patient child. I'm coming, I've told you.

He struggles to rise from his chair.

Kathleen's Voice Uncle Laurie! Open the door!

Lowry makes a desperate attempt to stand up and he stumbles into the side table, knocking over as he does so the 'Portrait of Ann'. He picks up the picture and gazes at it.

Kathleen's Voice Was Ann your girl friend Uncle Laurie?
Lowry (*Smiling to himself as he looks at the portrait*)
    She was my friend . . . and she was a girl.
Doreen's Voice But you never married her?
Lowry I never had the chance. She died while she was still very young. It all seemed to pass me by.

Lowry sits on the chair at the foot of the chaise longue as he did when his mother was alive.

He is still holding the Portrait of Ann. Now we can hear the clocks ticking in the silence.

Doreen's Voice It's a lovely picture. It's your mother isn't it? She was very beautiful. You do look like her.
Lowry She was a beautiful woman . . . so much talent . . . strangled by sickness.
Margaret Lowry's Voice She must have been very proud of your painting.
Lowry (*Evasive*)
She always . . . encouraged me to paint.

The doorbell again followed by a loud knocking. Then a montage of the girls' voices all calling to Lowry, followed by a sudden silence in which we can hear the Chopin polonaise in e flat minor.

Elizabeth Lowry's Voice Laurie. Are you there Laurie?
Lowry Yes mother. I'm here.
Elizabeth Lowry's Voice I've been on my own Laurie. Laurie, will you come and read to me?

The music is cut.

Lowry Yes mother. I'm coming.

As the lights fade to black out, we hear the music of Mozart's Requiem K 626.

THE END